# 101 Key SAT Words

**Rachel Kranz**

# CONTENTS

# Chapter 1

# Why Should I Prepare for the SAT Now?

You have lots of time to think about which college you'd like to attend, and your final decision may seem as if it's a long way off. Before you know it, however, you'll be a junior in high school preparing to take the SAT test! Now is the perfect time to become familiar with the types of questions and words that are commonly used in the English sections of this standardized test.

This book is crammed with 101 words that have appeared on previous SAT tests—and that's not all. Each word is introduced in a piece of writing, defined, and then used in a sample sentence. You can reinforce your understanding of the words by doing practice exercises at the end of each chapter. Also included are "Look-Alike Alerts" and "Sound-Alike Alerts," reminding you about words that look or sound similar but have completely different meanings; "Related Words," which is a list of other words that contain the same root word; "Fine-Tuning," which provides helpful hints for using words in their proper contexts; and "Root-Word Helpers"—explanations of root words. To further sharpen your word skills, you'll find three practice tests that simulate the types of questions you might find on the SAT.

If you want a high score on the English sections of the SAT, one of the most important things you can begin to do right now is improve your vocabulary. The best way to increase your word power is to read everything that interests you, from the sports section of the newspaper to science journals, from *Soap Opera Digest* to comic books. Of course, reading novels and plays and books about history, current events, and social issues wouldn't hurt either! The more you read, the more words you learn—and the more you get a feel for how words are used in different contexts. You might even have fun!

Although the SAT practice tests can give you an idea of what to expect, you should concentrate mainly on learning these 101 new words. Enjoy!

## Chapter 2

# Fighting Words

Have you ever had negative feelings about something and looked for strong words to express your disapproval? The words in this chapter will help you describe your critical feelings. Angry Angela used them to write an essay about the movies she likes—and doesn't like.

## Down with Violent Movies!

I *abhor* movies that are too violent. I wish I could *chastise* filmmakers who think it is necessary to portray car crashes and exploding buildings in every film. Some people argue that violence is the best way to appeal to today's audiences, but I *repudiate* that idea. Why does Hollywood *patronize* its audiences by assuming that we all have the attention span of a five-year-old? There is no need to *inundate* an audience with continual images of crime, murder, and mayhem.

Alfred Hitchcock, a great director in the 1940s and 1950s, would be the first to *censure* today's overly violent films. *North by Northwest,* one of Hitchcock's most thrilling films, features a hero who *vacillates* between being a brave man and being a coward. The villains try to kill the hero by means of an accident designed to *efface* all traces of their crime. Then they *coerce* the heroine into betraying the man she loves. The movie keeps viewers on the edge of their seats—but without showing the blood and gore so common in today's films.

Could you follow Angela's argument? Here are the SAT words she used to add force and vigor to her essay:

# 1. abhor *(verb)*—to hate, loathe, or detest

I *abhor* drivers who honk their horns early in the morning!

# 2. censure *(verb)*—to condemn in a stern fashion

The people who wrote the Bill of Rights *censured* the very notion of censorship.

LOOK-ALIKE ALERT: Don't confuse *censure* and *censor*. To *censor* something is to forbid it officially, usually by passing a law against it or by acting in some other official capacity. To *censure* is merely to express a criticism, usually from a position of authority. Thus Hitchcock, from his authoritative position as a great director of thrillers, could *censure*, or criticize, violence in modern movies, but he would never want to *censor*, or officially forbid, it, as he wouldn't want to restrict freedom of expression.

RELATED WORDS: *Censure* can also be a noun: When the drunken captain ran his ship aground, he faced *censure* by the company's board of directors.

3. chastise *(verb)*—to scold or criticize severely

Chaz *chastised* me when I borrowed his tie without permission.

4. coerce *(verb)*—to force someone against his or her will, either by means of physical force or through some kind of threat

My parents tried to *coerce* me into taking a college-prep course.

RELATED WORDS: A noun, *coercion,* comes from this verb: Actually, I wanted to take the course anyway, so no *coercion* was necessary.

5. efface *(verb)*—to erase or wear away

Years of wind and rain had gradually *effaced* the features of the statue.

LOOK-ALIKE ALERT: Don't confuse *efface* with *deface,* which means "to disfigure or spoil deliberately": A clever graffiti artist *defaced* the billboard.

6. inundate *(verb)*—to flood or overwhelm

When the disc jockey announced the giveaway, she was *inundated* with calls from eager listeners.

ROOT-WORD HELPER: *Inundate* includes the root word *unda,* which means "wave." To *inundate* something is like having a huge tidal wave sweep over it.

**7.** patronize *(verb)*—to talk down to or treat in a condescending way

Even though I'm younger than you are, you don't have to *patronize* me—I'm not stupid!

ROOT-WORD HELPER: *Patronize* comes from the root word *pater,* which means "father." If you *patronize* someone, you are behaving as though you were his or her wise, all-knowing father.

RELATED WORDS: A *patron* is someone who supports a person, a project, or a business. Although one sense of the word *patronize* is negative (to talk down to someone), another sense is positive (to be a customer or supporter): I like to *patronize* restaurants that donate their leftover food to soup kitchens.

**8.** repudiate *(verb)*—to reject, disown, or disclaim

When he was young, the candidate supported national health insurance, but now that he is older, he *repudiates* that position in favor of private health insurance.

RELATED WORDS: The noun that comes from this verb is *repudiation:* Mr. Pugh published a *repudiation* of the lawyer's claim in the Sunday paper.

**9.** vacillate *(verb)*—to move back and forth between two opinions or choices; to be unable to make a decision

Louis *vacillated* between asking Sarah or Susan to the dance; by the time he made up his mind, neither of them was available.

## Practice Questions

A. Match the word in the left column with its definition in the right column.

1. abhor
2. patronize
3. censure
4. repudiate
5. chastise
6. coerce
7. vacillate
8. efface
9. inundate

a. waver between two choices or positions
b. erase or wear away
c. criticize from an official position
d. scold
e. hate or despise
f. flood or overwhelm
g. talk down to or condescend
h. force
i. reject, disown, or disclaim

B. Choose the best word from the list to complete each sentence. Each word is used only once.

abhor     censure     chastise     coerce     efface
inundate     patronize     repudiate     vacillate

1. The School Board voted to _____ the principal for spending over the budget three years in a row.

2. Mr. Orton knew that if he could not _____ the charges against him, his career would be over.

3. It would be dangerous to _____; he needed to act quickly!

4. He stood up and said proudly, "I _____ the way the facts in this case have been distorted."

5. "I wish I could _____ this entire incident from my memory."

6. "I must _____ the School Board for acting without having all the facts."

7. He went on to _____ his listeners with a long list of confusing facts and figures.

8. *Is he trying to _____ us into taking his side?* wondered Ms. Hernandez, the School Board Chair.

9. "Don't _____ us!" she said aloud. "We understand the facts as well as you do!"

## Chapter 3

# Flattery Will Get You Everywhere!

Malcolm had to write an essay describing a person who was important to him, and he wanted to find just the right words to tell how much he admired his grandfather. Here's what he wrote:

## My Grandfather: A Person I Admire

I hold my grandfather in the very highest *esteem*. When he owned his hardware store, he was always *scrupulous* about making correct change and dealing fairly with every customer. He did many things to *ameliorate* conditions on Fourth Street, including spending his own money on two shade trees. He was always *magnanimous* about sharing his time and knowledge with others. For example, when some merchants decided to plant trees, Grandpa *facilitated* an arrangement with a local nursery and talked the owner into giving discounts to all the merchants.

Grandpa was an *eminent* member of our community who was asked to run for City Council more than once. He never *acquiesced* while he still had the hardware store. When he retired, however, he did volunteer work for Marcy Kim's campaign and was a *prolific* writer of leaflets.

Now Grandpa is in his eighties, and he spends most of his time sitting on his front porch with a *serene* but thoughtful expression on his face. I once asked him the secret of his *benevolent* attitude. He answered, "If you give people your best, they will probably give you their best in return."

Here are the SAT words Malcolm used:

**10.** acquiesce *(verb)*—to give in, or agree, peaceably in a reluctant way

I begged Mom and Dad to let me go to the party, and they finally *acquiesced* to my request.

FINE-TUNING: You can either *acquiesce,* or you can *acquiesce to.* Think of how you use the word *agree.* You can use *acquiesce* pretty much in the same way. Just remember that *acquiesce* has the sense of agreeing reluctantly, in order to keep the peace.

**11.** ameliorate *(verb)*—to make something better; to improve a bad situation

Amy worked hard to *ameliorate* the dreadful conditions at the county animal shelter.

FINE-TUNING: *Ameliorate* generally refers to a situation, a condition, or a problem. You might, for example, *improve* your grades or your chances of getting into college, but you wouldn't *ameliorate* them. If, however, you suddenly found yourself with a straight-A average, that might *ameliorate* a sticky situation with your teachers.

**12.** benevolent *(adjective)*—showing goodwill; being kindhearted or good-natured

The Immigrants' *Benevolent* Society gave out free food, clothing, and medical care to poor immigrants who needed help.

ROOT-WORD HELPER: *Benevolent* comes from the Latin word *bene,* which means "good." Related words include *benefactor* (one who does good for another), *benefit* (to enjoy a good result), *beneficiary* (one who has enjoyed a good result), and *benign* (kindly or not harmful): The *benign benefactor* made sure that her *beneficiary* would *benefit* from her *benevolence.*

RELATED WORDS: The noun that comes from this word is *benevolence.* The related adverb is *benevolently:* The queen smiled *benevolently.* Her *benevolence* was well known.

13. eminent *(adjective)*—distinguished; highly respected and well-known

The crowd rose to its feet, cheering the *eminent* politician.

LOOK-ALIKE ALERT: Don't confuse *eminent* with *imminent,* which means that something is about to happen: The *eminent* professor's arrival was *imminent.*

14. esteem *(noun)*—the high opinion in which someone is held

I admire Superman enormously, and my *esteem* is in no way lessened by the fact that kryptonite makes him weak.

RELATED WORDS: The word *esteem* is also a verb, meaning "to value very highly": I *esteem* Mrs. Johnson because she makes fractions fun.

# 15. facilitate *(verb)*—to make easier; to smooth the way

Pablo tried to *facilitate* the children's progress by clearing all the toys out of their way.

# 16. magnanimous *(adjective)*—generous; big-hearted and noble

In a typically *magnanimous* gesture, the doctor insisted on giving her nurse half the credit for the life-saving operation.

ROOT-WORD HELPER: *Magnanimous* comes from the Latin root *magna,* which means "large." Related words include *magnify* (to make larger), *magnificent* (large and wonderful), and *magnitude* (large size). Think of a *magnanimous* person as one who makes big, generous gestures, or someone with a large heart.

# 17. prolific *(adjective)*—producing a great deal; fertile, productive, fruitful

Linda is a *prolific* writer; I've seen her write twenty-five pages in a single day!

FINE-TUNING: A person or animal may be *prolific.* So may part of a person: a *prolific* mind, for example, may come up with six good ideas in five minutes. On the other hand, machines, methods, and approaches may be *fruitful* or *productive,* but they're not *prolific.* Think of *prolific* as "giving life to."

# 18. scrupulous *(adjective)*—thorough or ethical

Abraham Lincoln was so *scrupulous* that, according to legend, he once walked miles in the snow to return a few pennies.

RELATED WORDS: The adjective *scrupulous* comes from the noun *scruple,* which means "a moral or ethical principle that would cause a person to hesitate or doubt." The word is often used in its plural form: **The doctor's** *scruples* **would not allow her to take credit for work she did not do.**

# 19. serene *(adjective)*—calm, peaceful

As the sun came up over the isolated mountain lake, all was quiet and *serene.*

RELATED WORDS: The noun that comes from *serene* is *serenity:* It's difficult to achieve *serenity* when you're worried about passing a test!

## Practice Questions

A. Match the word in the left column with its definition in the right column.

1. serene
2. scrupulous
3. acquiesce
4. ameliorate
5. esteem
6. facilitate
7. magnanimous
8. prolific
9. benevolent
10. eminent

a. prominent, distinguished
b. to make better
c. to make easier
d. high regard
e. to agree reluctantly
f. calm, peaceful
g. fruitful, productive
h. generous
i. ethical, careful
j. kindhearted, showing goodwill

B. Change these insults into compliments! For every word or phrase in italics, write a word from the following list that has the opposite meaning. You should use each word from the list once. You might have to write an extra word, like *it,* or change *a* to *an.*

acquiesce          ameliorate          benevolent
eminent            esteem              facilitate
magnanimous        prolific            scrupulous
serene

1. I am happy to celebrate my friend Roger's birthday, because he is the most *stingy* person I know. _____

2. Roger is always ready to help out a friend. If you're trying to get something done and there's a way to *make it harder,* just call Roger! _____

3. And if you're in a difficult situation, a call to Roger will *worsen* things right away. _____

4. Roger is also extremely *dishonest* when it comes to sharing a piece of chocolate cake. _____

5. As for schoolwork, Roger is surprisingly *unproductive.* I've known him to write four pages in an hour!

   _____

6. Yet throughout it all, he remains *worried* and confident.

   _____

7. I am sure that he will one day be a(n) *little-known* scientist or politician. _____

8. All of us who are Roger's friends appreciate his *mean-spirited* attitude. _____

9. Our *low regard* for him should come as no surprise!

   _____

10. I see him motioning me to stop talking, and reluctantly, I will *refuse.* _____

## Chapter 4

# Not Quite This, Not Quite That . . .

Sometimes you need words to explain that you can't quite explain something! The words in this chapter are good for talking about things that change or things that are otherwise hard to pin down. Poetical Patrice wrote the following description of a morning when nothing seemed to go right—but she couldn't quite figure out why.

### Blue Monday

I woke up to the *banal* sound of my father calling up the stairs. "Come and get it!" he yelled. I was *dubious* about his offer. Into my room floated an *ambiguous* smell—was it burned toast, burned oatmeal, or burned bacon? This is a *chronic* problem in our house when my father cooks. As a result, I would prefer an *austere* meal of orange juice when he is at the stove. But my parents have a rule that I think is fairly *arbitrary:* they cook it, I eat it—no matter what it is.

When I came slowly down the stairs, the burned smell was growing stronger, but I felt extremely *reticent* to ask about it. Spread out over the counter was a *wanton* display of bowls and utensils.

"I have a *novel* idea," I wanted to say, "I'm going to fast today.

I'm not being *capricious*—I've thought this over carefully!" But I knew that saying this would be an *egregious* mistake.

In fact, my father served us all cold cereal, which was a great relief. But for the rest of the day, I felt an *amorphous* sense of dread that I couldn't quite explain. I knew I'd had a very narrow escape. But from what?

You can use these SAT words to talk about uncomfortable feelings and hard-to-describe situations:

**20.** ambiguous *(adjective)*—unclear, vague; having several different possible interpretations

I asked him whether he had sent me the valentine, but he gave me such an *ambiguous* reply that I'm still not sure.

RELATED WORDS: The noun related to *ambiguous* is *ambiguity:* I hate *ambiguity*—I like to know exactly where I stand!

**21.** amorphous *(adjective)*—without form, shape, or definition; sometimes also without character

The spilled oatmeal lay on the floor in an *amorphous* white blob.

LOOK-ALIKE ALERT: Can you tell the difference between *amorphous* and *ambiguous*? *Amorphous* means "shapeless" or "hard to define." *Ambiguous* means that something is confusing. When something is *amorphous,* you can't quite tell *what* it means. When something is *ambiguous,* you can't choose between all the different possible meanings. A shape or feeling can be *amorphous.* A statement, glance, facial expression, or intention can be *ambiguous.*

ROOT-WORD HELPER: The word *amorphous* comes from the root word *morph,* which means "shape," and the prefix *a,* which means "no."

**22.** arbitrary *(adjective)*—according to choice or impulse; without a rational reason

"Which cookie do you want?" said Martha. I made an *arbitrary* decision and pointed to the closest one.

**23.** austere *(adjective)*—stern, plain, severe, self-denying; without luxuries

The athlete maintained an *austere* routine: a low-fat diet, in bed by 9:30, and up with the sun to run ten miles each morning.

RELATED WORDS: The noun related to *austere* is *austerity:* Just the thought of such *austerity* makes me want to reach for the chocolate chip cookies and the remote control!

**24.** banal *(adjective)*—boring, ordinary, dull

Can you think of anything more *banal* than going shopping with your parents?

FINE-TUNING: The word *banal* is often used to suggest that something is worn out—that it was once interesting but now has become boring or ordinary. *Banal* can also be used to describe something that other people think is cool but that *you* know is about as far from cool as you can get. If you want to insult someone or something, *banal* is a good word to use.

RELATED WORDS: Two nouns are related to *banal*: *banality* (the state of being banal) and *banalities* (banal words or things): The *banality* of life in this town would be hard to describe. I thought the party would be fun, but the conversation was full of *banalities*.

**25.** capricious *(adjective)*—unpredictable, unsteady; changing on a whim

Jamal no longer liked to gamble, for now he understood that the cards could be *capricious*.

FINE-TUNING: *Capricious* is a somewhat playful word, but there is sometimes an undertone of criticism in it. A *capricious* person is an airhead—someone who is neither reliable nor steady. Sometimes being *capricious* can hurt people's feelings or upset their plans, and sometimes a *capricious* person can take advantage of his or her power: The child star made one *capricious* request after another, but no one dared to tell him no.

RELATED WORDS: The adverb that goes with this adjective is *capriciously*: Although Sam was acting *capriciously*, the waitress smiled patiently until he had made his dinner selection.

**26.** chronic *(adjective)*—long-standing, frequent; constantly recurring

My aunt's *chronic* arthritis has bothered her off and on for several years.

ROOT-WORD HELPER: The root of this word is *chron*, which means "time." So something that is *chronic* lasts over time. You may know some other words that have this root: *chronological* (in "time-order," or the order in which things happened) and *synchronicity* (the occurrence of two things at the same time). Did you know that the root *chron* comes from the Greek god *Kronos*, who was the father of Zeus in Greek mythology?

## 27. dubious *(adjective)*—doubtful, questionable

The ad for the new cereal made the *dubious* claim that Oatsies will double your energy and triple your strength.

ROOT-WORD HELPER: This word derives from the Latin word *dubitare*, which means "to doubt." If something is beyond doubt, you can say it is *indubitable*, or you can use the word *indubitably:* His facts and figures were *indubitable:* the meteor was indeed heading straight for Earth! *Indubitably,* he had spoken too soon, for the meteor proved to be a mere speck on the telescope lens.

## 28. egregious *(adjective)*—outstanding in a bad way; noticeably bad or foolish

The politician's most *egregious* error was to use foul language at the school assembly.

FINE-TUNING: Note that a person can't be *egregious*. But an action, idea, question, mistake, statement, display, or response can be.

ROOT-WORD HELPER: The Latin root for the word *egregious* is *greg*, which means "crowd." The basis for the word is:

*e(x)* (out of) + *greg* (crowd) = *egregious*
or something that stands out from the crowd

Other words that share this root are *gregarious* (friendly, sociable, crowd-loving), *aggregate* (a big group of something), and *congregation* (a group of people who are members of the same church).

## 29. novel *(adjective)*—new, original

I have a *novel* idea—let's *not* go to the mall today!

SOUND-ALIKE ALERT: You've probably heard the word *novel* used as a noun to mean a book-length work of fiction. Both the noun and the adjective come from the same idea—the French word *nouvel,* which, as an adjective, means "new" and, as a plural noun, "news." Originally, novelists pretended that their fictional characters were actually real people, and that the fictional story was actually a news report about these people.

## 30. reticent *(adjective)*—quiet, restrained; reluctant to speak

The coach encouraged the infield to chatter and heckle the opposing team, but for some reason, the players were *reticent.*

## 31. wanton *(adjective)*—reckless and unrestrained

That new city budget shows a *wanton* disregard for the needs of the poor.

## Practice Questions

A. Match the word in the left column with its definition in the right column.

| | |
|---|---|
| 1.  wanton | a.  unpredictable, unsteady |
| 2.  arbitrary | b.  unrestrained, reckless |
| 3.  banal | c.  shapeless |
| 4.  capricious | d.  lasting over time |
| 5.  chronic | e.  doubtful |
| 6.  ambiguous | f.  outstandingly bad |
| 7.  amorphous | g.  boring, ordinary |
| 8.  dubious | h.  severe, spare |
| 9.  egregious | i.  with more than one possible interpretation |
| 10. novel | |
| 11. reticent | j.  reluctant to speak |
| 12. austere | k.  new |
| | l.  without a logical reason |

B. Find the best word in the list to match each description of a person, place, or situation. Use every word in the list once.

| | | | |
|---|---|---|---|
| ambiguous | amorphous | arbitrary | austere |
| banal | chronic | capricious | dubious |
| egregious | novel | reticent | wanton |

1. A small, bare, unfurnished room lit only by a single unshaded lightbulb _____

2. A rock star who insists on having a special brand of bottled water in the dressing room—and then changes his mind and wants imported papaya juice

_____

25

3. A new study proving that people who listen to classical music live three times longer than other people

_____

4. A book in which you aren't sure who is the hero and who is the villain _____

5. A pool of spilled syrup _____

6. A huge, abandoned garden full of wildflowers mixed in with the garden flowers, with all the different plants growing every which way _____

7. A new type of toothbrush that brushes your teeth with sonar waves _____

8. A judge who lets one lawyer talk all she wants while charging the opposing lawyer with contempt of court for simply asking a question _____

9. The infestation of a house that has been full of termites ever since it was built, no matter how many times the exterminator comes _____

10. A person who is very shy about speaking up

_____

11. A song on the radio that you used to like, but that now you've heard over and over and over for the past several months _____

12. It's all you can do to keep from staring at Mr. Bigelow's very big nose. Then, just when you're safely saying good-bye, you hear yourself say, "Hope to see you again soon, Mr. Bignose." You hope Mr. Bigelow didn't hear— but you spoke so loudly, there's no way he missed it.

_____

## Chapter 5

# So You Want to Run for Office!

Have you ever noticed that certain words seem to come up again and again when people talk or write about political campaigns? Candidate Cal was running for class president, and he wanted to write a campaign speech that sounded like the ones he had heard on the TV news or read about in the newspaper. Here's what he wrote:

### Vote for Cal!

My fellow classmates, in these days of corruption and greed, I know that the very idea of an honest politician must seem old-fashioned—an *anachronism* that belongs in the pages of history and not before you today. But I promise that you can judge my honesty by the very highest *criteria.* If I am elected, I will not take an action because it is *expedient,* but only because it is right.

By now you must be wondering, who is this *intrepid* character who dares to come up and face the entire ninth-grade class of John F. Kennedy High School? Is he brave, or merely *quixotic?* Certainly an honest politician must seem like an *anomaly* in these days of bribe-taking and payoffs!

My fellow classmates, I ask you to curb your *propensity* to doubt me. I know that when a person repeats a promise over

27

and over again, that only *exacerbates* the tendency not to believe him. But I ask you to look at my record. I have always been a strong *proponent* of shorter lines in the cafeteria—and if elected, I will work to make those lines even shorter! I ask you to *juxtapose* my record with that of my opponent, who has actually been heard to say that she doesn't mind waiting fifteen minutes or more to eat lunch! Such disregard for the wishes of the majority of the student body amounts to nothing less than criminal *negligence.*

My fellow students, when election day comes, remember: a vote for Cal is a vote for honesty, shorter lunch lines, and a better way of life.

The following SAT words may come in handy, whether you're reading about politics or making a speech of your own.

## 32. anachronism *(noun)*—something that is out of place in time

The movie was supposed to be set in the Old West, but it was full of *anachronisms:* at one point, the hero pulled out a cell phone and called to order a pizza!

ROOT-WORD HELPER: Remember the word *chronic,* (lasting over time) from the previous chapter? The root word *chron* (time) shows up in *anachronism,* too. The prefix *an* means "outside of," and an *anachronism* is something that is "outside of [its proper] time."

## 33. anomaly *(noun)*—something that doesn't fit in with the norm or within a particular group

Everyone in my family would eat two or even three desserts, if given the chance. Since I hate sweets, this makes me an *anomaly.*

RELATED WORDS: The adjective form of this noun is *anomalous:* **The independent thinker is *anomalous* in a world of people who merely follow the trends.**

**34.** criteria *(noun)*—standards used to make a judgment

**What *criteria* should we use to choose players for the soccer team?**

RELATED WORDS: The word *criteria* is actually plural. When you are talking about a single standard, use the singular word, *criterion:* **My only *criterion* for a movie is that it has to star Brad Pitt!**

**35.** exacerbate *(verb)*—to make (a problem or condition) worse

**Luis had never liked Carlos—a feeling that was *exacerbated* when Carlos started dating Luis's ex-girlfriend.**

**36.** expedient *(adjective)*—practical; done to gain advantage

**It may not be right to flatter people, but sometimes it is *expedient.***

FINE-TUNING: Often the word *expedient* carries a negative connotation. On the one hand, there is the right, principled, perhaps unpopular course of action; on the other hand, there is the *expedient* thing to do, which is easier, more practical, and perhaps more helpful to one's career or social standing: **The City Council had the chance to improve education by raising taxes, but instead they did the *expedient* thing and cut the budget.**

# 37. intrepid *(adjective)*—brave, daring

The *intrepid* explorer hacked her way through the dense underbrush, ignoring the pythons that darted in front of her.

# 38. juxtapose *(verb)*—to place two things side by side, usually in order to compare them

*Juxtapose* the candidate's heroic war record and his strong commitment to peace, and you can see that his position does not spring from cowardice.

RELATED WORDS: The noun form of this verb is *juxtaposition:* Can you imagine a ballet about a football game? That would be a fascinating *juxtaposition!*

# 39. negligence *(noun)*—neglect, carelessness

When a person's carelessness results in the loss of human life, that is known as criminal *negligence.*

RELATED WORDS: The verb *neglect* (to fail to do something you were supposed to do), the noun *neglect* (the failure to do something you were supposed to do), and the adjective *negligent* (inattentive or careless) are all related words: Loulou *neglected* to feed her cat. Because of her *neglect,* the cat ran away. "How could I be so *negligent?*" Loulou cried.

# 40. propensity *(noun)*—strong natural tendency, preference

Parents seem to have a *propensity* for making suggestions and giving advice.

# 41. proponent *(noun)*—advocate

**Lydia says she's a *proponent* of exercise, yet her most strenuous activity is picking up the remote control.**

FINE-TUNING: The word *proponent* suggests a person who has argued in favor of something, or a person who has taken a firm position on an issue. You can't really be a *proponent* of your school team, for example, though you might be a team *supporter.* A politician, however, can be a *proponent* of gun control, in which case, he may debate an *opponent* of gun control.

# 42. quixotic *(adjective)*—overly idealistic; romantic and impractical

**You may think that banishing nuclear weapons is a *quixotic* idea, but I think it can be achieved with lots of work and commitment.**

ROOT-WORD HELPER: The word *quixotic* comes from the main character in the novel *Don Quixote,* by Miguel de Cervantes. In the novel, Don Quixote believes he is a medieval knight, and he travels around the countryside trying to rid the world of evil. Although Don Quixote is completely out of touch with reality, there is something moving about his idealism and romantic nature.

## Practice Questions

A. Match the word in the left column with its definition in the right column.

1. criteria
2. quixotic
3. juxtapose
4. propensity
5. exacerbate
6. intrepid
7. negligence
8. proponent
9. anachronism
10. anomaly
11. expedient

a. practical
b. to make worse
c. something out of time
d. advocate
e. something that doesn't fit
f. brave
g. standards
h. tendency
j. idealistic
k. to place two things side by side
l. carelessness

B. Replace the words in italics in the sentences below with a word from the list. Use each word from the list only once.
HINT: You might have to change *a* to *an* once or twice.

| | | | |
|---|---|---|---|
| anachronism | anomaly | criteria | exacerbate |
| expedient | intrepid | juxtapose | negligence |
| propensity | proponent | quixotic | |

1. If you *place side by side* the records of the two candidates, it's clear which one is better. _____

2. Not to vote for Councillor Goodguy would do so much harm to our city, it would amount to criminal *carelessness*.

   _____

3. It's true, Councillor Goodguy has a strong *tendency* to oversleep and miss council meetings. _____

4. It's also true that some of his ideas tend to be just a little *idealistic or romantic*. _____

5. But what are the *standards* by which we should judge a candidate today? _____

6. Councillor Goodguy is a(n) *person who doesn't fit in among* other politicians today. _____

7. His old-fashioned belief in honesty, fairness, and hard work make him a(n) *person who's living in the wrong time*.

   _____

8. Of course, some people say that he does not always do the right thing; sometimes he does the *practical, safe* thing.

   _____

9. They say his opponent, Mayor Superwoman, is a(n) *brave* fighter for justice. _____

10. They point out that she has always been a strong *advocate* of raising taxes—hardly a popular position.

    _____

11. But in Councillor Goodguy's opinion, raising taxes will only *worsen* the problems of this city. _____

# Practice SAT Test #1

Sentence Completions

Each of the following sentences has one blank or two blanks, representing a word or words that have been left out of the sentence. Each set of answer choices contains a selection of words or pairs of words that could be inserted into the blanks. Pick the answer choice whose word or words best completes the sentence.

Example:

An explorer may be intrepid on the outside but quite _____ on the inside.

(A) serene
(B) prolific
(C) fearful
(D) wanton
(E) indifferent

(answer: C)

Recommended time: 6 to 7 minutes

1. Though George claims to _____ the ballet, Jenny saw him buying tickets—and Lionel ran into him at the theater.

(A) esteem

(B) censure

(C) patronize

(D) inundate

(E) abhor

2. The millionaire was a capricious man, sometimes generous, but sometimes quite _____.

(A) magnanimous

(B) stingy

(C) benevolent

(D) bewildered

(E) genial

34

3. The lawyer charged that the actions of the judge were
   _____ and therefore _____.

(A) arbitrary . . . unfair
(B) austere . . . puzzling
(C) banal . . . surprising
(D) chronic . . . timely
(E) expedient . . . illegal

4. The treatment was harsh, even dangerous, and the doctor
   was uncertain whether it would cure the illness, or would
   actually _____ it.

(A) coerce
(B) chastise
(C) juxtapose
(D) exacerbate
(E) censure

5. Luis, an anomaly among his family of early risers, frequently
   went to bed _____.

(A) exhausted
(B) early
(C) dubious
(D) late
(E) confused

6. Is it likely that such a(n) _____ politician would stoop
   to lying?

(A) egregious
(B) prolific
(C) novel
(D) wanton
(E) eminent

7. Although the accountant was quite _____, she nonetheless was accused of _____.
(A) serene . . . ambiguity
(B) banal . . . benevolence
(C) scrupulous . . . negligence
(D) reticent . . . shyness
(E) dubious . . . certainty

8. The chairman was rather idealistic, indeed, even _____.
(A) amorphous
(B) reticent
(C) austere
(D) banal
(E) quixotic

9. Despite my best efforts to _____ the process, I succeeded only in getting in the way.
(A) facilitate
(B) exacerbate
(C) repudiate
(D) coerce
(E) censure

## Analogies

In each of the following questions you will find a related pair of words or phrases, followed by five more pairs of words or phrases. Choose the pair that most closely mirrors the relationship expressed in the original pair. Analogies are read as follows:

BOY: GIRL :: MALE: FEMALE
Boy *is to* girl *as* male *is to* female

**Example:**
TEARS: SADNESS::
(A)  dogs: kennel
(B)  frown: joy
(C)  respect: leader
(D)  smile: happiness
(E)  anxiety: anger
(answer: D)

**Recommended time: about 5 minutes**

10. ACQUIESCE: AGREE::
(A) support: disagree
(B) prove: disprove
(C) acquire: aggrandize
(D) ameliorate: worsen
(E) efface: erase

11. AMBIGUOUS: DOUBT::
(A) ashamed: pride
(B) joyous: happiness
(C) perilous: safety
(D) intrepid: fear
(E) trepidatious: courage

12. SHAPE: AMORPHOUS::
(A) fear: intrepid
(B) criteria: strict
(C) propensity: likely
(D) proponent: opposed
(E) anachronism: anomalous

# Chapter 6
# Make It Snappy!

Have you ever wanted to ask someone to make an explanation just a little shorter? The words in this chapter may seem long and complicated, but they can help you demand quickness and clarity. Impatient Ida wrote this letter to one of her teachers:

Dear Mr. Longwind:

A famous saying tells us that *"brevity* is the soul of wit," or, in other words, the wittiest people are the ones who say the least. I believe that everyone in our class would find your lessons more *coherent* if they were shorter. I'm not asking you to *circumscribe* or restrict your teaching. Indeed, I am trying to be *circumspect,* or at least cautious. But if I were to be *explicit,* I would have to say that your lectures are just too long!

Is there some *immutable* law that requires students to *scrutinize* the tiniest shades of meaning of every single word? Is it really necessary for you to spend half an hour explaining the *minuscule* difference between "ambiguous" and "amorphous"?

Mr. Longwind, I warn you: if you don't change your ways, revolution is *imminent!*

Your sincere student,
Ida

Take a look at the SAT words Ida used to make her point:

# 43. brevity *(noun)*—briefness

People who write comic books must be masters of *brevity*, since all their characters' words must fit into small speech balloons.

# 44. circumscribe *(verb)*—restrict

I don't want to *circumscribe* your response, but I will ask you to answer briefly and politely.

ROOT-WORD HELPER: The word *circum* means "around," while the word *scribe* means "write." To *circumscribe* literally means "to write around"—that is, to draw a line, or circle, around. Picture a wild animal standing in the midst of an open space. Now draw a circle around that animal and imagine someone building a cage where the circle is. The animal's movements have been *circumscribed,* or restricted.

# 45. circumspect *(adjective)*—cautious

When you are meeting people for the first time, it is wise to be *circumspect* in both your words and your actions.

ROOT-WORD HELPER: *Circum,* as we just learned, means "around," while *spect* comes from a root meaning "look." A *circumspect* person is one who "looks around" cautiously at his or her situation before acting or speaking.

# 46.
coherent *(adjective)*—arranged logically, fitting together well; clear

Pasquale made a thorough outline for his paper, so that his ideas would be *coherent* and clearly expressed.

FINE-TUNING: Usually this word is used to describe the written or spoken work: a *coherent* speech, book, or article. We sometimes also talk about *coherent* ideas (but never just one idea, since the word describes many pieces that fit together well). A person who speaks clearly and logically may also be called *coherent*. The opposite of this word is *incoherent:* This is the most *incoherent* article I have ever read; the author cannot form a simple sentence!

# 47.
explicit *(adjective)*—said clearly and fully, without question

The class disobeyed the teacher's *explicit* instructions to keep the test booklets closed until she said to open them.

ROOT-WORD HELPER: Look at how root words help make these meanings clear:

*ex* (out) + *plicit* (placed) = *explicit*
or said clearly; something that is *explicit* is stated outright

*im* (in) + *plicit* (placed) = *implicit*
or hinted at; something that is *implicit* is suggested without actually being said

RELATED WORDS: The opposite of *explicit* is *implicit,* which means "hinted at" or "suggested."

**48.** imminent *(adjective)*—about to take place; happening soon

Judging by those huge, dark clouds and the sound of thunder, I would say rain is *imminent!*

LOOK-ALIKE ALERT: Don't confuse *imminent* (about to happen soon) with *eminent* (prominent, well-known).

**49.** immutable *(adjective)*—unchangeable; used to describe something that cannot be changed

The *immutable* law of gravity tells us that what goes up must come down.

ROOT-WORD HELPER: The root in *immutable* is *mut*, which comes from a word meaning "change." *Im* in this case means "not." So something that is *immutable* is "not changeable." Other words with the root *mut* include *mutant* (something that has been changed from its original state) and *mutation* (the process of change).

**50.** minuscule *(adjective)*—tiny, very small

Amoebas are fascinating, but one needs a microscope to see these *minuscule* creatures.

ROOT-WORD HELPER: This word comes from the root *min*, which means "less" or "little." The word *miniature* (small) comes from the same root—so does the word part *mini*. A *mini*-lesson, for example, is a small, or *miniature*, lesson. For a lesson to be *minuscule*, however, it would have to be very, *very* small—say, one sentence long. Things that are *minuscule* are *really* tiny!

# 51.
scrutinize *(verb)*—to look at very closely; to study carefully

Take my advice and *scrutinize* that dog for fleas.

RELATED WORDS: The noun *scrutiny* means "close, careful study." Often—but not always—it refers to someone in authority looking at someone or something that is considered questionable: **The corrupt politician's budget came under careful** *scrutiny.*

## Practice Questions

A. Match the word in the left column with its definition in the right column.

1. circumscribe          a. unchangeable
2. scrutinize            b. clear, logical
3. coherent              c. stated directly
4. explicit              d. restrict
5. imminent              e. cautious
6. circumspect           f. study
7. brevity               g. tiny
8. minuscule             h. briefness
9. immutable             i. coming soon

B. Find the best word in the list to match each description of a person, action, thing, or situation. Use every word in the list only once.

| | | |
|---|---|---|
| brevity | circumscribe | circumspect |
| coherent | explicit | imminent |
| immutable | minuscule | scrutinize |

1. A careful person who always thinks before she speaks or acts

   _____

2. A clear, convincing speech that moves logically from one idea to the next _____

3. Directions that spell out exactly what to do

   _____

4. A party that is coming up the day after tomorrow

   _____

5. A speech that sums up everything the speaker wishes to say in only five minutes _____

6. A gnat that is so small, it can even get through a mesh screen _____

7. A new health inspector who spends hours examining every inch of the school cafeteria _____

8. The opinion of a person who insists that his mind is made up and is not going to change _____

9. A new rule that assigns each student to a specific seat in the lunchroom _____

# Chapter 7

# A Wild Party

Some words describe wild excitement, trickery, even danger! Daring Danny used some of those words in a letter to his pen pal telling about a Halloween party he attended.

Dear Maurice,

I'd like to tell you about the party I went to last week, but I feel somewhat *pessimistic* about being able to describe it. As I approached the place where the party was held, I heard a wild *cacophony* of frightening sounds. As I entered the dark, narrow hallway, I acted *nonchalant*, putting my hands in my pockets and whistling casually. Really, though, I felt a great deal of *trepidation*, even terror. If I were attacked, could I *evade* the danger? Could I leave this party with *impunity*, or would my hosts try to keep me here?

It took a certain amount of *temerity* for me to walk down the long, steep flight of stairs into the dark basement. As I made my way down the steps, I tried to imagine what scenes of *decadence* might await me. Would I witness *chicanery*—gamblers cheating each other, or beautiful women double-crossing handsome detectives?

I hate to use *euphemisms*, so I'll just come right out and

say it—I was a complete and total fool! All I saw was some kids from my school dancing and eating potato chips. One girl was dressed as a witch, but the rest of them weren't even wearing costumes! Oh, well. It was a fun party anyway!

Your friend,<br>Danny

If you ever need to describe an exciting scene, you may want to use some of the SAT words Danny used:

## 52. cacophony *(noun)*—a loud, harsh noise made up of sounds that don't blend very well

The students' violins, trumpets, flutes, and cymbals combined to create an ear-splitting *cacophony*.

ROOT-WORD HELPER: What do *telephone, symphony,* and *cacophony* have in common? You guessed it—they all use the root word *phon,* which means "sound." (Come to think of it, *phonics* shares that root, too.)

*telephone—tele* (far) + *phone* (sound)
a device that carries sound to faraway places

*symphony—sym/syn* (together) + *phone* (sound)
many different sounds coming together

*phonics*—a method of teaching people to read using the sounds of words

By the way, *cacophony* comes from the root *kakos,* which means "bad." So a *cacophony* is a "bad sound."

## 53. chicanery *(noun)*—trickery, deceit

The con man was ready to invent a new sort of *chicanery* at a moment's notice.

**54.** decadence *(noun)*—moral decay or decline

**My grandmother believes that sleeping past seven is a sign of *decadence*.**

ROOT-WORD HELPER: This word comes from the word *decay,* "to rot and fall apart," which can be used literally, to describe actual objects: **After only a few days, a corpse will start to *decay* unless it has been embalmed.** *Decadence,* however, is only used to describe *moral* decay. The related adjective is *decadent:* **My grandmother considers anyone who sleeps past seven to be *decadent*.**

**55.** euphemism *(noun)*—a pleasant or neutral word or expression used instead of an unpleasant, offensive, or obscene word or expression

**The politician didn't like talking about unemployment, so he used a *euphemism:* "temporary shortage of work opportunities."**

**56.** evade *(verb)*—to escape or avoid

**Paco tried to *evade* his father's pointed questions by changing the subject.**

RELATED WORDS: The noun *evasion* (escape, avoidance) and the adjective *evasive* (hard to pin down) can also be used: **Paco's *evasive* answers only made his father more suspicious.**

# 57. impunity *(noun)*—exemption; the ability to do something without punishment

A bad doctor who has a good lawyer may continue to practice medicine with *impunity*.

ROOT-WORD HELPER: The root word *pun* comes from the Latin verb *punire*, "to punish," and gives us lots of related words: How should society *punish* a doctor who makes a mistake? Some people say the *punishment* should be revoking his or her license. Others say the doctor should pay *punitive* damages (extra fees that are intended to punish the person who pays them).

# 58. nonchalant *(adjective)*—casual, unconcerned

Although Terry was terrified of asking Sandy to go on a date, he tried to look cool and *nonchalant*.

RELATED WORDS: The noun that goes with this adjective is *nonchalance*: The hero's *nonchalance* was unbelievable: even though he was tied hand and foot, suspended above a vat of boiling oil, and being dive-bombed by vampire bats, he managed to make a wisecrack about the villain's balding head.

# 59. pessimistic *(adjective)*—feeling gloomy or negative

*Pessimistic* people view a glass as half-empty, never as half-full.

RELATED WORDS: A person who has a negative outlook on life may be called a *pessimist*. The opposite of a *pessimist*, of course, is an *optimist*, one who feels *optimism* or has an *optimistic* view: I felt *optimistic* today, but your *pessimistic* attitude is starting to depress me!

# 60. temerity *(noun)*—recklessness, foolish boldness

Marta's *temerity* in talking back to the teacher resulted in her receiving detention.

# 61. trepidation *(noun)*—fear, anxiety

Filled with *trepidation*, I approached the snarling dog.

ROOT-WORD HELPER: Remember the word *intrepid?* That word means "without fear."

*in* (not) + *trepid* = no fear
*trepidation* = fear

Can you guess what the root word *trepid* means?
(HINT: The Latin verb *trepidare* means "to tremble.")

## Practice Questions

A. Match the word in the left column with its definition in the right column.

1. chicanery
2. trepidation
3. euphemism
4. evade
5. cacophony
6. pessimistic
7. nonchalant
8. impunity
9. decadence
10. temerity

a. avoid
b. polite word or phrase
c. harsh noise
d. feeling negative
e. boldness
f. fear
g. casual
h. trickery
i. moral decay
j. freedom from punishment

B. Change these words into their opposites! For every word or phrase in italics, write a word from the list that has the opposite meaning. You should use each word from the list only once.

cacophony     chicanery     decadence     euphemism
evade         impunity      nonchalant    pessimistic
temerity      trepidation

1. Yesterday I saw a movie called *The Con Man*, a story of *honest dealings* and elaborate scams.

   _____

2. The con man is a *nervous* man who always appears calm and confident. _____

3. Then he meets an honest woman who falls in love with him, but she is *optimistic* about her chances for happiness with such a scoundrel. _____

49

4. With great *timidity,* the con man sneaks into her house to talk with her alone. _____

5. He explains that he has always managed to *run right into* the arms of the law. _____

6. He also tells her that he always manages to carry out his scams with *punishment.* _____

7. She replies that she considers even the smallest lie a sign of *moral uprightness.* _____

8. He explains that he "liberates" money from people who don't need it, and she asks him not to use that *insulting word.* _____

9. Suddenly, the police arrive in a huge *pleasing noise* of sirens and barking dogs. _____

10. The man promises to reform, and with great *confidence,* he asks her to wait for him—and she agrees.

_____

## Chapter 8

# What's Black and White and Read All Over?

Jalisa used the words in this chapter to write a story for her school paper about the new sewage plant proposed for her town.

### Battle Heats Up Over Proposed Sewage Plant

A community meeting at the Springfield Town Hall was the site of a *virulent* battle over the sewage plant proposed for the corner of Twenty-Third Street and Water Lane.

Councilman Mark Miller called Juanita Lopez a dangerous *demagogue* who was more interested in building a personal power base than in serving the needs of Springfield. Miller claimed that Lopez was guilty of *hyperbole* when she provided statistics about the dangers of the new plant—statistics that he said are highly exaggerated. "This kind of careless fact-finding has an *insidious* effect on the community," he said.

Lopez called Miller a "*supercilious* snob" who was unwilling to listen to anyone's opinion but his own. "The day he was elected was a day that will live in *infamy*," she said.

Lopez, longtime president of United Citizens for the Environment, said she was unwilling to *malign* the City Council as a whole, or even to criticize it slightly. She pointed out that, for example, Councilman John Jarmusch is known as a dedicated, *zealous* fighter for the environment. "When Jarmusch talks, he really says something—it's not just empty *rhetoric,*" Lopez said.

When told of her remarks, Councilman Jarmusch refused to comment, saying that he did not want to *sanction* any criticism of fellow Council member Mark Miller. "Ms. Lopez is known for her *harangues* about the environment, but I think we should let the experts decide this issue," he said.

Councilwoman Trina Sossi later disagreed with all three of the others. "I don't trust the so-called experts and their mysterious *jargon,*" she said. "But I don't trust outsiders like Ms. Lopez, either."

Jalisa used these SAT words to describe the controversy:

## 62. demagogue *(noun)*—a leader who tells people what they want to hear and plays on people's prejudices

The *demagogue's* speech in favor of immigration restrictions relied on voters' fears of foreigners.

## 63. harangue *(noun)*—long, lecturing speech

After watching the latest Bruce Willis movie, Angela launched into a *harangue* about how tired she was of violent films.

RELATED WORDS: *Harangue* can also be used as a verb: If you continue to *harangue* me about my performance, I'm going to hang up.

## 64. hyperbole *(noun)*—wild exaggeration

George may have been guilty of *hyperbole* when he said that he was so hungry he could eat a horse.

FINE-TUNING: We can talk about *hyperbole* in general, or refer to a specific *hyperbole*. This term is often used in discussions of literary works, since many authors deliberately use *hyperbole,* often to create humor: **Mark Twain is a master of** *hyperbole.* **His dry, deadpan style makes even the most outrageous exaggeration sound plausible—until you think about it for a moment!**

## 65. infamy *(noun)*—evil reputation

The *infamy* of that gangster is known far and wide.

ROOT-WORD HELPER: As you've probably guessed, the root word of *infamy* is *fame,* which means "reputation." Here are some other related words:

*famous*—well-known for good reasons

*infamous*—well-known for bad reasons

## 66. insidious *(adjective)*—dangerous, slow, and subtle in its effect

Julie had an *insidious* habit of repeating wild rumors until everyone believed they were fact.

## 67. jargon *(noun)*—specialized language

The *jargon* of the carpenter's trade includes such terms as "biscuit" and "miter box."

FINE-TUNING: Technically, the word *jargon* means "specialized language." Over the years, however, the word has taken on a negative connotation, as though experts are using *jargon* either to keep secrets or to make simple things sound more complicated than they really are: **The doctor's *jargon* confused me so much that I didn't know whether I had a bad cold or a deadly disease.**

## 68. malign *(verb)*—to say evil, harmful things about someone

**Since Pablo was losing the argument, he decided to *malign* Bettina, calling her stupid, ugly, and a sore loser.**

RELATED WORDS: Two related adjectives are *malignant* and *malign,* which mean simply "evil": **My boyfriend doesn't have a *malignant* bone in his body, but my parents think he's *malign* because he keeps me out until midnight every night!**

## 69. rhetoric *(noun)*—speech that is persuasive but often insincere or meaningless in content

**Rosita's eloquent *rhetoric* could persuade non-swimmers to buy jet skis!**

FINE-TUNING: Originally, this word meant "the study of persuasive speech." Now, however, it almost always has a negative connotation, suggesting that the speech in question is insincere or meaningless: **That politician relies on *rhetoric* rather than her record to win elections.**

## 70. sanction *(verb)*—authorize, endorse, approve, allow

**I cannot *sanction* that type of behavior in my presence; if you have to use offensive words, please leave the room.**

RELATED WORDS: The noun form of this verb, usually used in the plural—*sanctions*—originally meant a reward for obedience but has come to mean a penalty for disobedience: **The City Council voted to institute** *sanctions* **against all businesses that discriminate in hiring.**

**71.** supercilious *(adjective)*—above it all; having a sense of superiority

**The successful movie star looked at the new actress with a** *supercilious* **smile and said, "Don't worry, dear, as soon as you fix that haircut and buy some** *real* **clothes, you'll be fine."**

ROOT-WORD HELPER: Remember that *super* means "above." A *supercilious* person feels that he or she is *above* all others.

**72.** virulent *(adjective)*—infectious, dangerous

**A** *virulent* **rumor can spread wildly and ruin a person's reputation.**

**73.** zealous *(adjective)*—enthusiastic and dedicated, sometimes overly so

**The detective was** *zealous* **in her pursuit of the truth, for she had to free an innocent man.**

RELATED WORDS: The related noun is *zealot,* which almost always has the negative sense of "fanatic": It takes a real *zealot* to keep preaching his beliefs when he knows no one is listening.

## Practice Questions

A. Match the word in the left column with its definition in the right column.

1. harangue
2. virulent
3. zealous
4. demagogue
5. insidious
6. jargon
7. infamy
8. malign
9. supercilious
10. rhetoric
11. sanction
12. hyperbole

a. infectious
b. insincere speech
c. fanatical
d. evil reputation
e. to say bad things about
f. superior, disdainful
g. specialized language
h. long, lecturing speech
i. sneaky
j. authorize
k. irresponsible leader
l. exaggeration

B. Choose the best word from the list to complete the sentence. Use each word once. You may have to change the form of some words slightly, adding an *s* or changing a verb to the past tense.

| | | | |
|---|---|---|---|
| demagogue | harangue | hyperbole | infamy |
| insidious | jargon | malign | rhetoric |
| sanction | supercilious | virulent | zealous |

1. My friend Wanda and I disagree about Mayor Bigshot. She thinks he is an irresponsible _____, while I think he is an effective, moving leader.

2. Wanda calls his long, critical speeches _____, whereas I always learn a lot from listening to him.

56

3. She thinks his opponent, Maria Pucci, is a good candidate, whereas I think Pucci is all _____ and no action.

4. Wanda thinks Mayor Bigshot is _____, but I think that if you are really superior to other people, it's difficult to hide it.

5. Wanda wonders how I can _____ Mayor Bigshot's long history of tax problems.

6. "I don't like to _____ anyone on personal grounds," she says, "but even you have to agree that his past record is pretty shady!"

7. I tell her that, considering the ridiculous and complicated _____ you find on tax forms, it's amazing that anyone can understand them.

8. In my view, to call someone a criminal just because he once had a tiny little problem with the IRS is the worst kind of

_____.

9. Wanda points out that Maria Pucci was a doctor at City Hospital for many years, and that she understands such _____, fast-spreading diseases as tuberculosis and pneumonia.

10. In Wanda's opinion, Dr. Pucci will be a dedicated, _____ advocate of better public health in our city.

11. Slowly but surely, Wanda is starting to win me over to her point of view. My father, who supports Mayor Bigshot, says that Wanda's influence on me has been _____.

12. Nevertheless, I am starting to think that the mayor's terrible reputation is his own fault and that his _____ is well deserved.

# Practice SAT Test #2

Sentence Completions

Each of the following sentences has one blank or two blanks, representing a word or words that have been left out of the sentence. Each set of answer choices contains a selection of words or pairs of words that could be inserted into the blanks. Pick the answer choice whose word or words best complete the sentence.

Example:
The movie star seemed casual, even _____, when greeted by her thousands of fans.
(A) wanton
(B) pessimistic
(C) zealous
(D) nonchalant
(E) scrupulous
(answer: D)

Recommended time: 6 to 7 minutes

1. Melissa tried to gather her scattered thoughts and give a(n) _____ answer.
(A) supercilious
(B) zealous
(C) insidious
(D) coherent
(E) explicit

2. The scientist had to use a microscope to inspect the _____ specimen.
(A) nonchalant
(B) minuscule
(C) circumspect
(D) immutable
(E) coherent

3. Max wished to be _____ so he used a _____.

(A) circumspect . . . euphemism

(B) explicit . . . hyperbole

(C) coherent . . . harangue

(D) supercilious . . . sanction

(E) pessimistic . . . metaphor

4. Laws governing libel and slander, which seem to _____ our freedom of speech, actually expand it.

(A) evade

(B) malign

(C) sanction

(D) scrutinize

(E) circumscribe

5. It was unusual for the reticent man to show such _____, but anger had made him brave.

(A) trepidation

(B) brevity

(C) decadence

(D) temerity

(E) chicanery

6. The music of Igor Stravinsky is an indescribable delight to some people, while to others, it is pure _____.

(A) decadence

(B) chicanery

(C) cacophony

(D) hyperbole

(E) rhetoric

7. Although the demagogue was a master of _____, she could no longer lie with _____, for the people were becoming suspicious.

(A) chicanery . . . ambiguity
(B) rhetoric . . . impunity
(C) hyperbole . . . infamy
(D) jargon . . . brevity
(E) decadence . . . euphemisms

8. Although revolution seemed to be coming soon, it was hardly _____; on the contrary, it would not arrive for another twenty years.

(A) explicit
(B) circumspect
(C) imminent
(D) virulent
(E) insidious

9. Despite the doctor's fears, the disease did not prove _____ but was actually rather mild.

(A) minuscule
(B) imminent
(C) explicit
(D) virulent
(E) insidious

## Analogies

Each related pair of words or phrases below is followed by five more pairs of words or phrases. Choose the pair that most closely mirrors the relationship expressed in the original pair.

**Example:**

JOY: SORROW::

(A) head: feet

(B) hat: shoes

(C) smile: happiness

(D) joyous: ecstatic

(E) blissful: miserable

(answer: E)


**Recommended time: about 5 minutes**

10. DECAY: GROWTH::

(A) exaggeration: hyperbole

(B) luminescence: light

(C) brevity: length

(D) rhetoric: demagogue

(E) euphemism: chicanery


11. EVADE: EUPHEMISM::

(A) confront: rhetoric

(B) malign: insult

(C) punish: impunity

(D) circumscribe: freedom

(E) scrutinize: conceal


12. DEMAGOGUE: RHETORIC::

(A) carpenter: hammer

(B) lawyer: judge

(C) leader: followers

(D) teacher: education

(E) president: vice-president

## Chapter 9

# The Scientific Method

You may find that some words are especially useful for talking about science—although you can certainly use them to talk about other topics! Scientist Samuel was supposed to observe some aspect of nature for one hour and write a report on what he noticed. Here's what he came up with:

## War and Peace

For several minutes, I noticed only the *mundane* activities that I assumed were normal for this time of day. Then, suddenly, a *plethora* of soldiers rushed from their homes to fight off a raid from their neighbors. What mysterious, *obscure* instinct had warned them of the danger? What *pandemic* alarm had spread throughout the entire population to alert them? I do not know; all I *do* know is that suddenly, the soldiers were *ubiquitous*, and everywhere I looked, they were fighting.

I found myself in something of a *quandary*, for if I moved, I might disturb the natural course of things, but if I stayed where I was, I might be attacked. I thought about enjoying a small *hiatus* from my work, but then I remembered the assignment: "Observe without interruption for an entire hour." Luckily, some general seemed to give an order that made its way down the *hierarchy* of command to reach even the lowliest soldier, for suddenly, the creatures disappeared. Their enemies had all been killed, and I admit I felt a *vicarious* sense of triumph on their behalf.

I really enjoyed this project, and I think it should serve as a *paradigm* for future assignments!

Did you guess that Samuel had been observing an anthill? Did you know—or could you guess—the meanings of the SAT words that he used? Here they are:

# 74. hiatus *(noun)*—break, interruption

Our basketball team was doing quite well until a leak in the gymnasium roof forced a *hiatus* in our practices.

FINE-TUNING: Usually, this word implies a long break in something that would normally continue. A planned five-minute break from studying does not qualify as a *hiatus,* but a broken computer or a lost textbook might force a *hiatus* of an hour or more.

# 75. hierarchy *(noun)*—a series arranged by rank, sometimes used to refer to the group of people in authority at the top of the ranking

In the *hierarchy* of our school, the sports heroes are at the top, with student council members a close second.

# 76. mundane *(adjective)*—ordinary, everyday

Normally, the walk to school was a *mundane* activity, but with Mei-Ling standing beside him, Brad felt as though he was walking on air.

ROOT-WORD HELPER: The Latin word *mundus,* "earth" or "world," is the root for our word *mundane.* Originally, the word was used to talk about earthly concerns as opposed to spiritual or heavenly issues: **To feed the body is *mundane*, but to feed the soul is a spiritual act.**

Now, however, the word has taken on the connotations of "daily," "boring," and "ordinary": **Cleaning my room, washing my hair, and other such *mundane* matters took up the whole morning.**

## 77. obscure *(adjective)*—vague, mysterious; not prominent or well-known

**The librarian suggested that we consult some *obscure* books that none of us had ever heard of.**

ROOT-WORD HELPER: The root for this word is the Latin *obscurus,* which means "to cover or conceal." Something that is *obscure* has been covered or hidden, whether literally (**The book was in a dark, *obscure* corner of the library**) or figuratively (**Her example was so *obscure*, I couldn't understand what she was trying to tell me**).

RELATED WORDS: There is also a verb *obscure,* which means to cover up or to conceal: **The criminal tried to *obscure* all signs that she had ever been at the scene of the crime.**

## 78. pandemic *(adjective)*—spread throughout a population

**When the stock market crashed, a *pandemic* sense of fear was felt across the nation.**

ROOT-WORD HELPERS: The root *dem* means "people," giving us *pandemic* and lots of other words:

*pan* (throughout) + *demic* = spread throughout the people
*epi* (over) + *demic* = spread over the people
*demagogue:* a leader who sways the people based on their prejudices
*democracy:* rule by the people
*demographic:* concerning the population (such as birth and death statistics)

# 79. paradigm *(noun)*—model

Mr. Douglass's excellent teaching methods have become a *paradigm* for biology teachers throughout the nation.

FINE-TUNING: Note that a system, a method, or an approach can be a *paradigm,* but a person cannot be. A person, however, can be a *paragon,* which also means "model" or "shining example": **Mr. Douglass is a *paragon* among biology teachers.**

# 80. plethora *(noun)*—surplus, overabundance

Tisha opened the door of the crowded antiques store and saw a *plethora* of mysterious but beautiful objects.

# 81. quandary *(noun)*—puzzling situation, often one in which there seems to be something wrong with every solution; state of uncertainty

Bart was in a *quandary:* if he left now, he would just be on time for soccer practice, but he would miss Jennifer's phone call.

# 82. ubiquitous *(adjective)*—found everywhere

In the spring and summer, pigeons are *ubiquitous,* but in colder weather, you can't find a single one.

# 83. vicarious *(adjective)*—felt or experienced secondhand

When her son won the trophy, Ms. Patridge felt a *vicarious* sense of triumph.

RELATED WORDS: The adverb that goes with this adjective is *vicariously:* If you live *vicariously* through reading books and watching movies, you may never get hurt—but you might miss a lot of fascinating real-life experiences!

## Practice Questions

A. Match the word in the left column with its definition in the right column.

1. vicarious       a. ordinary
2. hiatus       b. found everywhere
3. mundane       c. affecting most people
4. obscure       d. break
5. plethora       e. felt through another
6. quandary       f. mysterious
7. hierarchy       g. surplus
8. ubiquitous       h. ranking
9. pandemic       i. model
10. paradigm       j. puzzling situation

B. Circle the two words or phrases that come closest to conveying the meaning of the word on the left (in italic type).

1. *mundane* ordinary extraordinary unusual everyday
2. *plethora* surplus shortage enough excess
3. *quandary* mystery challenge confusion task
4. *ubiquitous* widespread unusual common unique
5. *paradigm* model example paragon paradox
6. *vicarious* vicious precarious secondhand once-removed
7. *hiatus* status break session interruption
8. *hierarchy* commander chief ranking order
9. *obscure* obscene dark confusing secure
10. *pandemic* pantheon widespread epidemic endemic

## Chapter 10
# You Seem Nice, But . . .

Have you ever noticed that there may be several ways to describe the same quality? Some of these descriptions put a positive spin on things; others are more negative. Playwright Penelope played with positive and negative words when she wrote a dialogue in which a girl tries to describe her new boyfriend to her skeptical best friend:

### What Kind of Guy Is He???

LUZ: Oh, Miriam, I just met this wonderful guy. He's so *frugal!*

MIRIAM: You mean, he's cheap. Luz, you are so *impetuous.* You're always getting into tough situations before you think them through.

LUZ: (in a *querulous,* complaining tone) You never like anybody I go out with.

MIRIAM: Well, you go out with weird guys. The last one talked nonstop from the moment I met him to the time we said good night, three hours later! He was such a *garrulous* person!

LUZ: So he was a little *loquacious.* What's wrong with that? I certainly prefer that to a guy who is so *laconic* that he can barely open his mouth.

**MIRIAM:** It wasn't just that he talked too much. Everything he said was so *inane.* I've never heard such a silly conversation in my entire life!

**LUZ:** Well, don't hold back. Tell me what you really think.

**MIRIAM:** Some people think I'm *impudent,* but I'm just trying to be honest.

**LUZ:** But you hate everybody! You're such a *misanthrope!*

**MIRIAM:** I like *you.* You're my best friend—I don't want to see you get hurt. But I'll wait until I meet this guy before I make any more judgments.

**LUZ:** Thank you.

Here are the SAT words Miriam and Luz used to make their points:

## 84. frugal *(adjective)*—careful with resources; unwilling or unable to spend money

When Carlos first moved to New York City, he led such a *frugal* life that he would walk three or four miles rather than pay to take the subway.

RELATED WORDS: The noun that goes with *frugal* is *frugality* (thrift; economy). The adverb is *frugally* (in a thrifty or sparing manner): When people don't have much money, they must live *frugally. Frugality* is a virtue, but being excessively cheap is probably a fault!

## 85. garrulous *(adjective)*—talkative

The *garrulous* old man kept us in the store for hours telling us about his experiences in World War II.

**86.** impetuous *(adjective)*—impulsive, acting without thinking

As she passed the shop window, Lorna made the *impetuous* decision to run in and buy a purple-and-green polka-dot bathing suit.

RELATED WORDS: The adverb that goes with this adjective is *impetuously* (rashly or hastily, without thinking): Lorna threw her money down on the counter *impetuously*, and a moment later she was walking out of the shop with her new purchase.

**87.** impudent *(adjective)*—rude in a bold, daring way, often to one's superiors or elders

Donna knew some damaging information about her boss—so she could afford to be *impudent* to him without fear of losing her job.

RELATED WORDS: The related noun is *impudence;* the related adverb is *impudently:*
"Young man," said Ms. Horton to the five-year-old boy, "how dare you stick your tongue out at me? I don't believe I've ever seen such *impudence!*"
The boy smiled *impudently* and stuck his tongue out still further.

**88.** inane *(adjective)*—silly, senseless

Some older people believe that most of today's teenagers are *inane,* giggling nitwits who don't have a serious thought in their heads.

RELATED WORDS: The related noun is *inanity* (the condition of being silly, or a silly thing to say or do) or *inanities* (many silly things to say or do). There is also an adverb, *inanely* (in an inane, silly, senseless manner):
"The Cold War was a fight between rival drug companies over marketing a cough syrup," said Iris *inanely.*
If I have to listen to any more of her *inanities,* I'll scream.
I haven't heard such *inanity* in a long time.

# 89. laconic *(adjective)*—expressing as much as possible in as few words as possible

Although he is a *laconic* man in public, he is quite talkative when he's with close friends.

RELATED WORDS: The adverb that goes with this adjective is *laconically,* which implies mystery or "having deeper meaning": Cal smiled *laconically* and said nothing at all.

# 90. loquacious *(adjective)*—talkative

The *loquacious* young woman on the bus had soon told her entire life story to her seatmate.

FINE-TUNING: *Loquacious* is a synonym for *garrulous.* In fact, the two words are practically interchangeable, although *garrulous* might be a bit more critical, suggesting someone who runs on at the mouth. *Loquacious* has more the connotation of a talkative, friendly person.

# 91. misanthrope *(noun)*—someone who hates or distrusts everybody

The new boy in Paula's history class just sat there with a grouchy look on his face. Was he a *misanthrope,* or just shy?

FINE-TUNING: There are many ways of being a *misanthrope.* Some *misanthropes* just don't like being around people, and so they may seem quiet, isolated, or shy. Others are vocal and aggressive, complaining about how people are no good, or saying that they won't let anyone take advantage of them! The important thing to remember is that a *misanthrope* doesn't like people in general, even if he or she makes an exception of one or two friends.

# 92. querulous *(adjective)*—complaining, whining

Sue Ellen is the most *querulous* member of our study group: she always has to find something to complain about.

## Practice Questions

A. Match the word in the left column with its definition in the right column. Note that two words will get the same definition.

1. frugal
2. impetuous
3. misanthrope
4. impudent
5. querulous
6. garrulous
7. loquacious
8. inane
9. laconic

a. talkative
b. using few words
c. rude
d. complaining
e. someone who hates people
f. silly
g. impulsive
h. thrifty

B. In each word group below, cross out the word that does not belong.

1. pleasant   polite   impudent   considerate
2. loquacious   laconic   garrulous   talkative
3. silly   inane   empty-headed   intelligent
4. easy-going   quiescent   cheerful   querulous
5. free-spending   frugal   extravagant   wasteful
6. careful   impetuous   impulsive   hasty
7. philanthropist   people-lover   misanthrope   helper

## Chapter 11

# Getting Specific

It's important to get right to the main idea. Often you can find a single specific word to take the place of a long string of more general words. Editor-in-chief Ernest used some specific words in this humorous editorial he wrote complaining about the food in the school cafeteria.

### How Long Must We Suffer?

It is an *enigma* to me why the food in the school cafeteria is always so bad. Every day my classmates and I wait for the *inexorable* arrival of lunch hour with dread. When I was younger, I sometimes felt a fleeting, *ephemeral* sense of hope that today would be different. (Though even then, hope would die as soon as I smelled the weird fumes coming from the kitchen!) Now, however, I understand that the cafeteria's output is not *erratic*. On the contrary, the quality is always bad.

Our cafeteria food seems to be cooked by people who believe that taste, smell, and nutritional value are *superfluous*. The only thing that counts is appearance, specifically color. Yesterday, for example, we were greeted with an *eclectic* menu: green glop, yellow slop, and red gunk.

Is there no escape, no way to *extricate* ourselves from this dilemma? I myself am *partial* to the theory that the cafeteria should be closed and we should order pizza every day.

One thing is clear: If school food does not improve soon, those in the lunch line may turn into a *recalcitrant* mob, unwilling to listen to reason. And we'd be only too happy if someone told us, as Marie Antoinette told a similar mob in Paris long ago, "Let them eat cake!"

Ernest used these SAT words to say exactly what he meant:

## 93. eclectic *(adjective)*—being carefully chosen from many different sources

After hours of preparation, J.D. was ready with an *eclectic* collection of music for the dance. He had some rap, some rock, some house music, and some funk—but only the best of each.

## 94. enigma *(noun)*—mystery; a riddle whose answer is hard to figure out or may not actually exist

To our drama class, the director remained an *enigma*. We could never figure out what she wanted us to do, why she said the things she did, or whether she liked our performances.

RELATED WORDS: The adjective form of the word is *enigmatic* (mysterious, puzzling). The adverb is *enigmatically* (in a mysterious, puzzling way):
"Life is like a bowl of cherries," said the wise man *enigmatically.*
"Really?" said the student. "That statement is far too *enigmatic* for me to understand. Why is life like a bowl of cherries?"

## 95. ephemeral *(adjective)*—fleeting; here one moment and gone the next

To the lovesick heroine, happiness seemed as *ephemeral* as the morning dew.

**96.** erratic *(adjective)*—unpredictable; differing from what is expected

Mark's *erratic* behavior has me worried. One day, he sends me flowers and swears that he loves me. The next day, he won't even talk to me when I call him on the phone.

> ROOT-WORD HELPER: The basis of *erratic* is the Latin root *err,* "to wander." An *erratic* person "wanders all over the place," behaving strangely or in unusual ways.

**97.** extricate *(verb)*—to get free of an entanglement or a difficult situation

When the minister caught us stealing quarters from the collection plate, I wondered how we would *extricate* ourselves from such an embarrassing predicament.

> RELATED WORDS: If you can't extricate yourself from something, you are *inextricably* caught, or caught "so that you cannot be freed or separated": The crooks' destinies were *inextricably* linked from that day forth. Where one went, the other had to follow.

**98.** inexorable *(adjective)*—relentless, inflexible; showing no mercy

Amanda tried to talk her way out of the punishment, but her father was *inexorable.* She had broken curfew, and now she would be grounded.

FINE-TUNING: Be careful not to confuse *inexorable* with *inevitable* (inescapable, unavoidable). Use *inevitable* when you want to focus on the impossibility of evading or escaping from something. Use *inexorable* when you want to focus on the thing itself—its merciless, unyielding quality:

The judge was *inexorable*. She insisted on imposing the heaviest possible penalty.

If you commit a crime in this state, punishment is *inevitable*. Sooner or later, you will be caught and sentenced.

**99.** partial *(adjective)*—biased; favoring one side over another

The judge seemed *partial* toward the prosecuting attorney, so the lawyer for the defense filed a complaint.

RELATED WORDS: Another common meaning of the same word is "incomplete, referring to a *part* as opposed to the whole": Parker gave only a *partial* answer, while Connie gave a more complete response.

There is also the word *impartial*, meaning "unbiased, evenhanded, *not partial*" (in the first sense of the word *partial*). The adverb form is *impartially* (fairly): The lawyer wanted the case to be re-tried before a more *impartial* judge. Judges are supposed to treat both lawyers *impartially*, showing no favoritism to either side.

**100.** recalcitrant *(adjective)*—tough to control; defiant of authority

The king realized that soon he would be facing a *recalcitrant* group of peasants, hungry and desperate, who would even battle armed guards in their efforts to storm the palace.

**101.** superfluous *(adjective)*—extra, unnecessary

My parents insisted on being home when I gave my party, even though I tried to convince them that their presence was *superfluous.*

ROOT-WORD HELPER: The prefix *super* means "above." You can think of something *superfluous* as being "over and above" what's actually needed.

## Practice Questions

A. Match the word in the left column with its definition in the right column. Note that one word takes two definitions.

1. enigma              a. unavoidable

2. erratic             b. biased

3. superfluous         c. unnecessary, extra

4. partial             d. chosen from many sources

5. eclectic            e. get out of something

6. ephemeral           f. hard to control

7. recalcitrant        g. incomplete

8. extricate           h. mystery

9. inexorable          i. unpredictable

                       j. fleeting, lasting only a short time

B. Mark the sentences below *S* for *sense* or *N* for *nonsense*, depending on how the italicized word is used.

_____ 1. The *enigma* was so simple, a child could understand it.

_____ 2. The *partial* behavior of the judge was easy to understand, for she was known as one of the most fair, evenhanded judges in the county.

_____ 3. The room was decorated in an *eclectic* style: the sofa was an old-fashioned rose color with huge, soft cushions; but the armchair was ultra-modern, made from stainless steel.

_____ 4. His friendship was so *ephemeral*, Jenna knew she could count on it for the rest of her life.

_____ 5. Leanne could not *extricate* herself from the delightful party, so she remained there willingly.

_____ 6. Peter never does anything half-heartedly, so his commitment to win the game was *partial* and heartfelt.

_____ 7. Martina tried several times to fix her hair, but one *recalcitrant* strand kept escaping from the clip.

_____ 8. The presence of the doctors at the accident scene was completely *superfluous*, and José was grateful to see them there.

_____ 9. Tim's mood was quite *erratic*, for one moment he was on top of the world, and the next, he was in the depths of despair.

_____ 10. LaToya had put off studying for so long that she dreaded the *inexorable* day of the test.

# Practice SAT Test #3

Sentence Completions
Each of the following sentences has one blank or two blanks, representing a word or words that have been left out of the sentence. Each set of answer choices contains a selection of words or pairs of words that could be inserted into the blanks. Pick the answer choice whose word or words best complete the sentence.

Example:
The photographer tried to make his pictures clear and sharp, yet critics called them _____.

(A) stunning

(B) blurry

(C) striking

(D) dramatic

(E) upsetting

(answer: B)

Recommended time: 6 to 7 minutes

1.  Although many newspaper columnists applauded Eleanor Roosevelt's interest in public affairs, many others _____ her for interfering in the president's business.

(A) repudiated

(B) coerced

(C) effaced

(D) chastised

(E) patronized

2. Marcy _____ dishonesty, yet she could not decide to leave the man who had lied to her.

(A) vacillated

(B) facilitated

(C) coerced

(D) abhorred

(E) esteemed

3. The economic conference came up with a proposal designed to _____ the participation of developing nations in the world market, a proposal that the developing nations wholeheartedly endorsed.

(A) facilitate

(B) exacerbate

(C) circumscribe

(D) evade

(E) censure

4. In the novel *Jane Eyre,* the character Mr. Rochester is presented as a somewhat _____ man who seems to look down on most of the people he knows.

(A) magnanimous

(B) banal

(C) capricious

(D) scrupulous

(E) supercilious

5. The architect adopted a rather _____ style, featuring bare white walls; uncarpeted floors; and plain, almost severe furniture.

(A) austere

(B) arbitrary

(C) serene

(D) ambiguous

(E) amorphous


6. Adolf Hitler was known as a brilliant _____ who could sway crowds of people with his fiery rhetoric.

(A) paradigm

(B) quandary

(C) anachronism

(D) anomaly

(E) demagogue


7. T. S. Eliot is one of the most influential poets of the twentieth century; indeed, it would not be _____ to call him "the father of twentieth-century poetry."

(A) infamy

(B) hyperbole

(C) jargon

(D) rhetoric

(E) negligence

8. When the _____ music of the composer Arnold Schoenberg first burst onto the scene, most people did not understand it and considered it mere _____.

(A) mundane . . . decadence

(B) reticent . . . chicanery

(C) egregious . . . pessimism

(D) eclectic . . . enigma

(E) novel . . . cacophony

9. In 1918, a particularly _____ and deadly strain of influenza quickly spread around the world, taking on almost _____ proportions.

(A) insidious . . . inane

(B) virulent . . . pandemic

(C) quixotic . . . imminent

(D) inexorable . . . immutable

(E) recalcitrant . . . obscure

10. After World War I, many nations joined to _____ war, yet the peace they achieved was only _____.

(A) malign . . . ubiquitous

(B) scrutinize . . . expedient

(C) sanction . . . partial

(D) ameliorate . . . erratic

(E) repudiate . . . ephemeral

## Analogies

In each of the questions below you will find a related pair of words or phrases, followed by five more pairs of words or phrases. Choose the pair that most closely mirrors the relationship expressed in the original pair.

**Example:**
CAPTAIN: SHIP::
(A) dog: wolf
(B) ringmaster: circus
(C) teacher: college
(D) chef: waiter
(E) parent: child
(answer: B)

Recommended time: about 10 minutes

11. BREVITY: LOQUACIOUS::

(A) honor: sleepy

(B) humor: funny

(C) punctuality: late

(D) privacy: protected

(E) politeness: respectful

12. HARANGUE: COMPLIMENT::

(A) help: complement

(B) harbinger: complete

(C) speech: rhetoric

(D) scolding: praise

(E) argument: resolution

13. HIERARCHY: EQUALITY::

(A) temerity: bravery

(B) propensity: tendency

(C) proponent: supporter

(D) impunity: punishment

(E) trepidation: nervousness

14. LACONIC: GARRULOUS::

(A) lackadaisical: garbled

(B) impetuous: zealous

(C) necessary: superfluous

(D) dissatisfied: querulous

(E) frugal: miserly

15. INUNDATE: PLETHORA::

(A) evade: honesty

(B) juxtapose: strategy

(C) extricate: politeness

(D) malign: insults

(E) acquiesce: disagreement

16. MISANTHROPE: CHARITY::

(A) euphemism: directness

(B) enigma: energy

(C) hiatus: vacation

(D) hierarchy: status

(E) demagogue: rhetoric

17. SCRUTINIZE: MINUSCULE::

(A) chastise: impudent

(B) repudiate: circumspect

(C) believe: dubious

(D) admire: prolific

(E) evade: explicit

18. CHRONIC: TEMPORARY::

(A) garrulous: loquacious

(B) impudent: capricious

(C) coherent: disorganized

(D) intrepid: fearless

(E) prominent: eminent

19. WANTON: NONCHALANCE::

(A) calm: criteria

(B) magnanimous: generosity

(C) inane: wisdom

(D) obscure: clarity

(E) frugal: extravagance

20. VICARIOUS: SUBSTITUTE::

(A) benevolent: misanthrope

(B) circumspect: circle

(C) ubiquitous: hyperbole

(D) magnanimous: beneficiary

(E) mundane: paradigm

## Answer Key

Chapter 2—pages 11–12
A. 1-e, 2-g, 3-c, 4-i, 5-d, 6-h, 7-a, 8-b, 9-f
B. 1. censure 2. repudiate 3. vacillate 4. abhor 5. efface 6. chastise
7. inundate 8. coerce 9. patronize

*Explanation for B:*
*Sentences 1 and 6.* You might think that *chastise* would work for the first sentence—and the sentence does make sense that way. If, however, an official body votes to *chastise* someone, what it has done is *censure* that person. So *censure* would be a more precise answer—and more like the answer that would be considered right on the SAT.

Likewise, in Sentence 6, Mr. Orton certainly can *censure* the School Board, but as an individual, he would be more likely to *chastise* them. Once again, the correct SAT answer will be the word that most closely fits the sentence, even if other answers also make sense.

*Sentence 2.* Although Mr. Orton might wish he could *efface* the charges against him, that isn't the way the word is usually used. *Repudiate* means "to reject"; *efface* simply means "to erase." Usually people *repudiate* charges, offers, positions, proposals, and claims. They *efface* memories, traces, and physical images.

*Sentence 3.* Although several words from the list might make sense, the SAT-type clue in the sentence—"to act quickly"—tells you that the missing word means the *opposite* of acting quickly; in this case, the word is *vacillate*.

*Sentence 4.* It's possible that *repudiate* could go in the blank here, but again, that isn't the way the word is usually used. *Abhor* is a better fit. Besides, *repudiate* is a perfect fit for Sentence 2, so by the process of elimination, another word probably fits better in Sentence 4.

*Sentence 7.* Although either *chastise* or *patronize* makes a certain kind of sense here, the SAT-type clue is "long list." The mention of all those confusing facts and figures should bring up the idea of *inundate,* since people are usually *inundated* with a lot of something.

*Sentence 8.* Although *chastise* would make sense here, *coerce* (force) is more simple and direct.

*Sentence 9.* Although *chastise* would make sense here, too, *patronize* fits the SAT-type clue. Ms. Hernandez wants Mr. Orton to realize that "We understand the facts as well as you do!" If he does *not* realize this, then he is talking down to, or *patronizing,* them.

Chapter 3—pages 17–18
A. 1-f, 2-i, 3-e, 4-b, 5-d, 6-c, 7-h, 8-g, 9-j, 10-a
B. 1. magnanimous 2. facilitate 3. ameliorate 4. scrupulous 5. prolific 6. serene
7. eminent 8. benevolent 9. esteem 10. acquiesce

Chapter 4—pages 25–26
A. 1-b, 2-l, 3-g, 4-a, 5-d, 6-i, 7-c, 8-e, 9-f, 10-k, 11-j, 12-h
B. 1. austere 2. capricious 3. dubious 4. ambiguous 5. amorphous 6. wanton
7. novel 8. arbitrary 9. chronic 10. reticent 11. banal 12. egregious

*Explanation for B:*
*Sentence 1. Austere* means "stern, plain, severe, self-denying." The word "bare" should have tipped you off.

*Sentence 2.* The words "changes his mind" should have been your clue. A *capricious* person is someone who changes his or her mind on a whim.

*Sentence 3.* You might have been side-tracked by the word "new" and chosen *novel.* But remember always to read the whole clue. The most important thing about the study being described is not how new it is, but how unlikely it is that it could be correct. If you realized what the study was saying, you would go on to choose *dubious,* "doubtful."

*Sentence 4.* Here the words "aren't sure" might have made you think of "doubtful"—but again, you have to read the whole sentence. The overall uncertainty—not knowing which character is the hero and which the villain— is the very essence of *ambiguity,* and so should have led you to *ambiguous.*

*Sentence 5.* If you picture a pool of spilled syrup, you know it has no shape. From there it's a short step to choosing *amorphous,* "shapeless."

*Sentence 6.* Here the words "mixed in" and "growing every which way" should have pointed you toward *wanton,* which means "unrestrained."

*Sentence 7.* Here the word "new" should point you to *novel.* Sometimes an obvious word is the clue—but sometimes it's a trick! You have to get a feeling for the whole sentence, and then see where the clue is.

*Sentence 8.* In this sentence, you need to get a picture of what's being described before you can choose the word. The description of letting one person do one thing and another person do something else should suggest the word *arbitrary.* Also, *arbitrary* is often a word used about authority figures. The authority figure of the judge might have helped you choose the correct word, too.

*Sentence 9.* Here the words "ever since it was built"—going on over time—should have pointed you to *chronic.*

*Sentence 10.* The words "shy about speaking up" are practically a straight definition of *reticent.*

*Sentence 11.* The words "used to like" and "over and over and over" should help you think of *banal,* "boring." The sense of the song being played over time might have made you think of *chronic,* but that word is more often used to describe a situation or a problem, not something specific, such as a song.

*Sentence 12.* "There's no way he missed it" should help you choose *egregious.* Another clue is the fact that the item describes someone making a mistake—a circumstance that goes with *egregious.* You might have been misled into thinking that this situation was *ambiguous,* especially when "you hope Mr. Bigelow didn't hear you." But when the sentence says "There's no way he missed it," then the situation is no longer *ambiguous* (open to many different interpretations).

Chapter 5—pages 32–33
A. 1-g, 2-j, 3-k, 4-h, 5-b, 6-f, 7-l, 8-d, 9-c, 10-e, 11-a
B. 1. juxtapose 2. negligence 3. propensity 4. quixotic 5. criteria 6. anomaly
7. anachronism 8. expedient 9. intrepid 10. proponent 11. exacerbate

Practice SAT Test #1—pages 34–37
1-E, 2-B, 3-A, 4-D, 5-D, 6-E, 7-C, 8-E, 9-A, 10-E, 11-B, 12-A

*Explanations for Answers to Practice SAT Test #1:*
1. The sentence sets up an opposite through the word "though": whatever George claims must contradict the fact that Jenny saw him buying tickets and Lionel ran into him at the theater. Therefore, *esteem* and *patronize* don't work. And *inundate* simply doesn't make much sense. That leaves a choice between *censure* and *abhor.* Since *censure* means "to express an official criticism of," that choice is a bit more far-fetched than *abhor,* which simply means "to hate."

2. Here, you have to understand that *capricious* means "easily changeable." So whatever word fits in the blank must be the opposite of "generous." Only *stingy* fits that description. The other words either mean something close to "generous" or have a completely different meaning.

3. In this sentence, it's the word "therefore" that gives you the clue. *"Arbitrary* and therefore *unfair"* makes sense. None of the other pairs go together in the same way.

89

4. Here, look at the sense of the sentence. What would a "harsh, even dangerous" treatment do to an illness? You also get a second clue—what the treatment does is the opposite of "cure the illness." Since *exacerbate* means "make worse," that's the word that fits. You can't really *chastise, coerce, juxtapose,* or *censure* an illness, and none of these words are the opposite of "cure."

5. This question requires you to know the meaning of *anomaly*—something that doesn't fit in with its surroundings. If Luis doesn't fit into his family, the early risers, how would he go to bed? *Late* is the only word that contradicts "early" so directly. It's true that Luis might go to bed *exhausted* or even *confused* or *dubious,* but these words don't express the idea of *anomaly.* And *early* is simply incorrect; going to bed early would not make Luis "an anomaly among his family of early risers."

6. What type of politician would *not* be likely to "stoop to lying"? The word *eminent* is the only one that fits. An *egregious* or *wanton* politician might lie. *Prolific* and *novel* don't have anything to do with the sentence.

7. Notice the clue word "Although." It tells you that the two words in the pair must contradict each other. Which two words are opposites? *Scrupulous/negligence* and *dubious/certainty* are both pairs of opposites, so the answer might be either one of them. But why would an accountant be *accused* of certainty? Since that pair doesn't make any sense, the first pair, *scrupulous/negligence,* must be the answer.

8. Here, the clue words are "indeed, even," which tell you that the answer must be a stronger version of "idealistic." Only *quixotic* fits that requirement.

9. The clue word here is "Despite." It tells you that the answer will be the opposite of "getting in the way." All of the answer words mean something like "getting in the way" except one—*facilitate,* which means "to make easier."

10. E—To *acquiesce* means to *agree.* Only two words can be plugged into that pattern: To *efface* means to *erase.*

11. B—Someone who is *ambiguous* is full of *doubt.* Someone who is *joyous* is full of *happiness.*

12. A—Something that has no *shape* is *amorphous.* Someone who has no *fear* is *intrepid.*

Chapter 6—pages 42–43
A. 1-d, 2-f, 3-b, 4-c, 5-i, 6-e, 7-h, 8-g, 9-a
B. 1. circumspect 2. coherent 3. explicit 4. imminent 5. brevity 6. minuscule
7. scrutinize 8. immutable 9. circumscribe

*Explanation for B:*

Are you remembering to look for the SAT clue—the word or words that tell you which is the right answer? Here are the clues that should have tipped you off for this quiz:

*Sentence 1:* The careful person is a cautious person—and since *circumspect* means "cautious," that's the correct answer.

*Sentence 2:* It's true that a clear speech might be short, but if you chose *brevity*, you were ignoring the clue word "logically." That word should have tipped you off that *coherent* is the correct answer.

*Sentence 3:* The clue words "exactly" and "spell out" should have made you think of *explicit*. Again, such directions might be brief, but if you chose *brevity*, you were missing the clue words.

*Sentence 4:* "Coming up the day after tomorrow"—that is, soon—should make you think of *imminent*, which means "coming up soon." It's likely that the date of the party is *explicit* and that it probably won't change *(immutable)*, but those answers ignore the obvious clue, which focuses on how soon the party is happening.

*Sentence 5:* Here "only five minutes" should make you think of briefness, or *brevity*. If "sums up" made you think of *coherent*—that is, a logical summary—you were missing the more important clue that focused on how short the speech was.

*Sentence 6:* The key word here, of course, is "small," which should make you think of *minuscule*.

*Sentence 7:* The clue here is "examining every inch." This kind of close, careful examination should make you think of *scrutinize*. It's true that health inspectors make rules that might *circumscribe* the kinds of things that go on in a cafeteria, but that isn't what the phrase describes.

*Sentence 8:* The words "not going to change" should make you think of *immutable*.

*Sentence 9:* The idea of assigning students to specific seats tells you that the students are restricted. The idea of restriction should help you to think of *circumscribe*, which means "to restrict."

Chapter 7—pages 49–50
A. 1-h, 2-f, 3-b, 4-a, 5-c, 6-d, 7-g, 8-j, 9-i, 10-e

B. 1. chicanery 2. nonchalant 3. pessimistic 4. temerity 5. evade 6. impunity
7. decadence 8. euphemism 9. cacophony 10. trepidation

## Chapter 8—pages 56–57
A. 1-h, 2-a, 3-c, 4-k, 5-i, 6-g, 7-d, 8-e, 9-f, 10-b, 11-j, 12-l
B. 1. demagogue 2. harangues 3. rhetoric 4. supercilious 5. sanction 6. malign
7. jargon 8. hyperbole 9. virulent 10. zealous 11. insidious 12. infamy

*Explanation for B:*
Don't forget to look for the SAT clue—the words or ideas that help you choose
the right answer. Here are the clues that should have tipped you off for this quiz:

*Sentence 1:* Since a *demagogue* is an "irresponsible leader," those two words in
this sentence should have helped you choose correctly.

*Sentence 2:* It might have been tempting to choose *rhetoric* for this answer—
and you wouldn't exactly have been wrong. But because of the word "critical,"
*harangues* is a more specific answer. Not all *rhetoric* is critical—but all
*harangues* are.

*Sentence 3:* Here is another clue to getting the right answer for Sentence 2.
*Harangues* doesn't make any sense here but *rhetoric* does. If you used *rhetoric*
here, you would have to find a different word for Sentence 2—and the only
other word that even comes close to making sense is *harangues*.

*Sentence 4:* This sentence is tricky, because many words on the list might fit if
you stopped reading at the blank space. If you go on to read the whole sentence,
however, you realize that because of the word "superior," the only answer that
can be correct is *supercilious*.

*Sentence 5:* Here, the word *malign* might make sense—but only if you didn't
know that the narrator supports Mayor Bigshot. You would hardly be likely to
*malign* (say evil, harmful things about) a person that you supported. You would
be far more likely to *sanction* (approve) such a person.

*Sentence 6:* Here, Wanda, a strong opponent of Mayor Bigshot, criticizes him
again. She is *maligning* him.

*Sentence 7:* Some people may think that *rhetoric* would be a good choice here,
and it is definitely a strong runner-up. It has, however,  two strikes against it: 1)
It was already used in Sentence 3, and since *jargon* doesn't work at all in that
sentence, the process of elimination tells you it's likely to work here. 2) The key
word, "understand," fits better with *jargon*, which implies difficult, complicated
language, than with *rhetoric*, which implies insincere, meaningless—but

possibly simple—language. This is a case where both answers might be right, but *jargon* is simply better.

*Sentence 8:* Here, getting the right answer depends on your ability to put together the words "criminal" and "tiny little problem." If the problem really is tiny, then it is an exaggeration, or *hyperbole,* to call someone a criminal because of it.

*Sentence 9:* Here is another sentence where there are two acceptable answers— *insidious* and *virulent*—but where one answer is better. *Insidious* means "sneaky" and "subtle," but there is nothing in the word that suggests either "fast" or "slow." *Virulent,* however, includes the idea of "fast-spreading" plus the idea of "deadly," or "dangerous." The word "fast-spreading" should have pointed you toward *virulent.*

*Sentence 10:* Here, the word *zealous* is used as a synonym for the word *dedicated.* Although many different adjectives on the list might have gone with the noun *advocate,* only the adjective *zealous* goes with the word *dedicated.*

*Sentence 11:* The words "slowly but surely" should make you think of *insidious.* It's possible that the narrator's father could have called Wanda's influence *malign* (evil), using *malign* as an adjective and not as a verb. But since a *malign* influence can be either slow or quick, and an *insidious* influence only happens "slowly," *insidious* is the better choice.

*Sentence 12:* The words "terrible reputation" should tell you that *infamy* is the correct answer.

Practice SAT Test #2—pages 58–61
1-D, 2-B, 3-A, 4-E, 5-D, 6-C, 7-B, 8-C, 9-D, 10-C, 11-B, 12-A

*Explanations for Answers to Practice SAT Test #2:*
1. The words "gather her scattered thoughts" should point you toward the answer that most clearly expresses that idea: *coherent.* Although *explicit* might make sense, it doesn't fit as well as *coherent* does.

2. The clue word "microscope" should point you to the idea of smallness: *minuscule.*

3. The word "so" tells you that the two words in the correct pair are closely linked: you use one in order to make the other happen. The closest links are between *circumspect* and *euphemism.*

4. Here, note the words "seem" and "actually" in the sentence, which tell you that the answer will be the opposite of the word "expand." The word *circumscribe* is the opposite of *expand.*

5. The word "unusual" tells you that the answer will be almost opposite of the word *reticent*. The word "but" indicates that the correct answer will be similar to *brave*: Thus, *temerity* is the best choice.

6. The word "while" tells you to look for an opposite. In terms of music, what word is the opposite of "delight"? That word could only be *cacophony*.

7. Here, your strategy is to find the first word of a pair that fits, so you can eliminate some answers. What might a *demagogue* be master of? Any of the words might fit except *decadence*, of which no one is really a "master." Now move on to the second half of the pair in the other four choices. Look for a word that expresses what the demagogue wants to do, but can "no longer" do. Saying "she could no longer lie with *brevity*" or with "*infamy*," doesn't make much sense. A demagogue might want to lie with *ambiguity*, but she would much rather lie with *impunity*, which is a better answer.

8. The words "on the contrary" tell you to look for an opposite for "not . . . for another twenty years"—in other words, "after a long while." The opposite of that is *soon*, or *imminent*.

9. Here again, look for an opposite. The disease was not something "harsh"; it was "actually rather mild." So you want a word that means harsh—that is, *virulent*.

10. C—*Decay* is the opposite of *growth*, the way *brevity* is the opposite of *length*.

11. B—You *evade* something by means of a *euphemism*, just like you *malign* someone by means of an *insult*.

12. A—The most important tool of a *demagogue* is *rhetoric*, just like the most important tool of a *carpenter* is a *hammer*.

Chapter 9—pages 67–68
A. 1-e, 2-d, 3-a, 4-f, 5-g, 6-j, 7-h, 8-b, 9-c, 10-i
B. 1. ordinary, everyday 2. surplus, excess 3. mystery, confusion 4. widespread, common 5. model, example 6. secondhand, once-removed 7. break, interruption 8. ranking, order 9. dark, confusing 10. widespread, epidemic

Chapter 10—page 73
A. 1-h, 2-g, 3-e, 4-c, 5-d, 6-a, 7-a, 8-f, 9-b
B. The words that don't belong: 1. impudent 2. laconic 3. intelligent 4. querulous 5. frugal 6. careful 7. misanthrope

Chapter 11—pages 78–79
A. 1-h, 2-i, 3-c, 4-b and g, 5-d, 6-j, 7-f, 8-e, 9-a
B. 1-N, 2-N, 3-S, 4-N, 5-N, 6-N, 7-S, 8-N, 9-S, 10-S

Practice SAT Test #3—pages 80–86

1-D, 2-D, 3-A, 4-E, 5-A, 6-E, 7-B, 8-E, 9-B, 10-E, 11-C, 12-D, 13-D, 14-C, 15-D, 16-A, 17-A, 18-C, 19-B, 20-D

*Explanations for Answers to Practice SAT Test #3:*

1. The word "Although" should cue you to look for the opposite of *applauded* which is *chastised*. The word *repudiated* would work, but it does not oppose *applauded* as directly as does *chastised*.

2. The word "yet" should cue you to look for an opposite. Marcy must have a bad feeling about dishonesty, in order for the word "yet" to make sense here. The only answer that expresses this bad feeling is *abhorred*.

3. How would the developing nations feel about their participation in the world market? Would they want to *exacerbate* it (make it worse), *circumscribe* it (limit it), *evade* it (avoid it), or *censure* it (officially condemn it)? Or would they want to *facilitate* it (make it easier)? The only word that makes sense is *facilitate*.

4. The clue here comes at the end of the sentence, "who seems to look down on most of the people he knows." The word that best expresses this meaning is *supercilious*. Mr. Rochester may have the other qualities described by the other answer choices, but the sentence asks you to choose a word that matches "who seems to look down. . . ."

5. Again, look at the description in the sentence: "bare white walls; uncarpeted floors; and plain, almost severe furniture." The only choice that fits this description is *austere*.

6. What is the term for someone "who could sway crowds of people with his fiery rhetoric"? The term is *demagogue,* so that is the right choice. Even if one of the choices had been *dictator,* and you knew Hitler was a dictator, that would not be the best choice. Only *demagogue* fits the clue at the end of the sentence.

7. Here, you might start by eliminating the choices that do not work. *Infamy* means "evil reputation," so this word doesn't make much sense. *Negligence*—"carelessness"—doesn't make much sense either. Although *jargon* and are possible, *hyperbole*—"exaggeration"—is more precise. *Rhetoric* sincere or meaningless speech," while *jargon* means "specialized *hyperbole* is a particular kind of speech—exaggerated speech— and, therefore, a better answer than the others.

8. For the first part of the sentence, look at the words "burst onto the scene." The word *novel*—new—best fits that clue. Music that people did not understand might be called *chicanery* (trickery), *enigma* (mystery), or *cacophony* (meaningless noise), but the word "mere" suggests that you should choose the most negative word possible—which is *cacophony*.

9. The key words here are "spread around the world." That should point you to the second word, *pandemic*. Does the first half of that pair—*virulent*—fit with the clue word "deadly"? Yes, so that pair must be the answer.

10. Here, your best strategy is to try both halves of each pair. ". . . nations joined to *malign* war . . ."—that makes sense. But "the peace they achieved was only *ubiquitous*" (appearing everywhere) does not make sense. The process of elimination leads you to the final choice: they *repudiated* (rejected) war but their peace was only *ephemeral* (short lasting).

11. C—A person who practices *brevity* cannot be *loquacious;* a person who practices *punctuality* cannot be *late*.

12. D—A *harangue* is the opposite of a *compliment,* just like a *scolding* is the opposite of *praise*.

13. D—Where there is *hierarchy,* there cannot be *equality;* where there is *impunity,* there cannot be *punishment*.

14. C—A person who is *laconic* cannot be *garrulous;* a person who is *necessary* cannot be *superfluous*.

15. D—You *inundate* someone with a *plethora* of things; you *malign* someone with *insults*.

16. A—A *misanthrope* is opposed to *charity;* a *euphemism* is opposed to *directness*.

17. A—You need to *scrutinize minuscule* things; you need to *chastise impudent* people.

18. C—If something is *chronic,* it is the opposite of *temporary;* if something *coherent,* it is the opposite of *disorganized*.

19. B—A *wanton* person displays lots of *nonchalance;* a *magnanim* displays lots of *generosity*.

20. D—A *vicarious* act requires a *substitute;* a *magn* beneficiary.